GW00471935

CLASSIC RECIPES
FROM THE GREEK ISLAND
OF KEFALONIA

Series: COOKERY
Title: CLASSIC RECIPES FROM THE GREEK ISLAND OF KEFALONIA
Writer: TASSIA DENDRINOU
Photographs: MICHALIS KOUVIDIS
English translation: PANAYOTA VLAHOPOULOU – DANIELLE BOWLER

Copyright © Tassia Dendrinou
Copyright of photos © Michalis Kouvidis
Copyright © 2001:
LIVANI PUBLISHING ORGANIZATION S.A.
96, 98 Solonos Street, 106 80 Athens, Tel.: 3600398, Fax: 3617791
http://www.livanis.gr

ISBN 960-14-0403-1

CLASSIC RECIPES
FROM THE GREEK ISLAND
OF KEFALONIA

TASSIA DENDRINOU

CLASSIC RECIPES FROM THE GREEK ISLAND OF KEFALONIA

Photographs:
MICHALIS KOUVIDIS

LIVANIS PUBLISHING ORGANIZATION
ATHENS 2001

Series: COOKERY
Title: CLASSIC RECIPES FROM THE GREEK ISLAND OF KEFALONIA
Writer: TASSIA DENDRINOU
Photographs: MICHALIS KOUVIDIS
English translation: PANAYOTA VLAHOPOULOU – DANIELLE BOWLER

Copyright © Tassia Dendrinou
Copyright of photos © Michalis Kouvidis
Copyright © 2001:
LIVANI PUBLISHING ORGANIZATION S.A.
96, 98 Solonos Street, 106 80 Athens, Tel.: 3600398, Fax: 3617791
http://www.livanis.gr

ISBN 960-14-0403-1

As I am a naturally ambitious person I hope this book goes well. I feel it is imperative for me to dedicate this book to one person only, to Panos, my husband. He has been by my side since 1973. He puts up with all my whims and outbursts. He supports all my decisions, right or wrong. He indulges me extravagantly. He supports me and gives me strength. And above all, he has the courage, after so many years, to still be in love me.

Contents

Introduction

Hello! I'm Tassia. Many of you know me, others don't. For all of you I'll try to take you on a guided tour of my life, to present you with a kind of curriculum vitae, so to speak.

I was born in March 1959 in Cefalonia where I have lived all my life in the northern part of the island and specifically, after 1971, in Fiscardo.

I was brought up in a household where my parents were occupied for the first twelve years of my life, in farming and stock-raising – after that we opened up the restaurant.

Our house, like the whole of the area, had no electricity until 1971 and during the first years of my childhood to go to Argostoli, which was the capital of the island and 52km away, took four hours, or even longer, by bus. Conditions, which in this day and age, when everything works at the touch of a button, seem primitive.

There is one thing I remember well in this house: there was cooked food every day and often many people at our table, because my father, who is a fan of good food and wine, believed that one could not enjoy these without good company.

Bread was baked in the oven. Wine was in barrels in the cellar below. Cheese and yogurt were always homemade. Some of it was used to cover the family's needs and the rest was sold to support the family income.

It was because I grew up in this household that two things have stayed with me: the first is that I adore cooking and the second that I can never enjoy good food without company. I believe that cooking, apart from some basic rules, is love, imagination and artistry. To me, a real home is not one filled with nice furniture and expensive carpets, but one which smells wonderfully of the cooking of food or the baking of cakes, and where people gather around the table or the fireplace.

It was because of this love for cooking (I had no specialized knowledge) and more generally my love for people, who came by our restaurant either as customers or friends, that together with my family we became known for our tavern which has existed since 1971 and which for its first 22 years was open every day, all day long.

My long-standing acquaintance with Giota Livani resulted, after a very long telephone conversation in August, 2000, in Mrs Livanis' suggestion for a cookery book containing recipes of food cooked my way, many of which have many fans.

I must point out that I'm a person who has made very quick decisions about important issues of my life.

Let me mention two or three examples. When we were considering buying our store in Fiscardo, at a time when our finances were tight, it took me only 2-3 minutes to reach a decision and tell my brothers that we would buy it.

When, a few years ago my brother, who was finishing his studies in America, rang me one morning to ask me if we wanted to go over to America as there were special offers on domestic tickets, I called him back within the hour to tell him that we would go – again it was not a very good time for us financially.

When my daughter announced that she had failed her university entry exams it was only a matter of minutes before I was searching for a way for her to go to England.

I have mentioned the above to stress the fact that although Mrs Livanis' phone call took place on August 3rd, my decision to accept took me almost two months.

I don't exactly know why I needed so long to answer. Probably because I considered such a move to be a great responsibility. I hope it will succeed.

My last reservation vanished when I asked for one and only one condition, which was immediately agreed to: that the beginning of the book would contain a tribute to Fiscardo.

Fiscardo is for me the most beautiful and picturesque place in the world. It has the rare advantage of combining sea and mountains. It was blessed by God and remained intact during the 1953 earthquake. It has a rare natural harbour.

During the summer months it combines two worlds: opulence in all its glory and naturalism. Fiscardo is the place where my family and many others made a name for themselves professionally.

I believe, that because of this tribute to Fiscardo, you will love this place, and that, those of you who haven't come here yet, will be tempted to do so very soon.

For those of you who already know and love Fiscardo and I'm truly in a position to know this as you come here so often – keep it in your file.

Kefalonia

Kefalonia is the largest of the Ionian islands and is situated at the entrance of the Patraikos gulf (gulf of Patras), between Zakinthos and Lefkada. A narrow channel separates it in the northeast from Ithaca, the island that has connected its name to the wandering Odysseus. The two islands make up the prefecture of Kefalonia with Argostoli as its capital.

Kefalonia is a mountainous island dominated by Ainos, one of the ten Greek forests and surrounded by endless bays and picturesque seashores. Only here can you find the black fir tree and the miniature wild horses, known as the Ainos horses. The highland slopes of the island are suitable for cultivating vines that produce Robola, a unique white wine.

The animal and plant worlds are not the only rare features of Kefalonia. It is endowed with geological phenomena. Kounopetra, a rock which moves rhythmically in the sea, is one of the unsolved mysteries of our century, while lake Akoli kept the secret of its depth for years. Large amounts of sea water disappear into the swallow-holes of Argostoli and travel through subterranean channels to re-emerge on the eastern side of the island, in the area of Sami, where there are some wondrous caves, such as the cave of Drogarati with stalactites, stalagmites, marvellous acoustics and the extraordinarily beautiful cave-lake of Melissani.

The small snakes in Arginia and Markopoulo and the flowers of St. George in Pastra are two more features, which added to the island's phenomena make it all the more strange and unique.

Mitikas

PREVEZA

Vonitsa

Cape Giropetra

LEFKAS

Palairos

Karia

1589

LEFKAS IS.

Mt. Elati
1158

MEGANISION

Akarnanian Mountains

Ag. Petros

Spartohorion

Kalamos

Cape Lipso

KALAMOS IS.

Cape Doukaton

ARKOUDION IS.

KASTOS IS.

Cape Melissa

Cape Dafnoudi

Fiscardo

Stavros

ATOKOS IS.

ITHACA IS.

Cape Atheras

Strait of Ithaca

ITHACA

Atheras

1131

Sami

Kominarata

Dilinata

Cape Ag.

KEFALONIA IS.

Lixourion

ARGOSTOLI

Mt. Ainos

Tsanata

1628

Geroyobos

Vlahata

Scala

Cape Liakas

Cape Moüda

Cape Skinar

Cape

Kill

Ano Volimai

P. Killinis

Katastarion

Cape
Trikeri

ZAKYNTHOS

756

Cape
Krioneri

Strait of Zakyr

Ag. Leon

ZAKYNTHOS

ZAKYNTHOS IS.

Maharadon

Historical flashback

The island has been inhabited since Paleolithic times. The peninsula of Fournia is rich in tools and flints dating back to the Paleolithic age. During the Classical period, Fiscardo just like the whole of the peninsula of Erisos came under the dominion of Sami, one of the four ancient towns of Kefalonia (Sami, Krani, Pali, Proni).

In Roman times, the port of Fiscardo, played an important part in the transport and exchange of materials and culture between the Italian peninsula and Greece. The place named "Panormos" with its temple of Apollo mentioned in literary sources of the time is today identified by most researchers as Fiscardo. This belief is also substantiated by the existence of a Roman cemetery (2nd-4th century AD) discovered along the seafront of the present-day settlement. Many graves have been found to contain opulent funeral gifts. The sarcophagi with reliefs (the abduction of Persephone) are of special interest.

The large three-aisled early Christian basilica near the lighthouse on the peninsula proves the existence of a powerful Christian community in the settlement. Although derelict today, the large semi-circular apse of the sanctum is discernible but only the two double-storey towers of the west side survive.

In the 12th century Kefalonia became the centre of marine enterprise between the Byzantines and the Normans. It also became a target for Norman raids, the most significant being that of 1084, led by Robert Wiscardo who died the following year in the port of Panormos, which was named Fiscardo from then on.

During Venetian rule there was a lot of maritime trade in Fiscardo, especially during bad weather, when the port of Asos, despite its unassailable fortress, provided no safe mooring. At the same time the inhabitants of neighbouring villages used it for smuggling raisins. Because of

the great danger from pirates, the settlement only developed in the late 18th century. The first houses were fortified manor houses, few of which have survived to this day. Fiscardo acquired its current look the following century particularly after the union of the Eptanisa (the Ionian Islands) with mainland Greece (1864).

Fiscardo

The port of Fiscardo is in the municipality of Erisos, the most northerly part of the island, and at the entrance to the channel of Ithaca. It is an exceptionally safe and leeward port protected to the north by a narrow peninsula on which a lighthouse dating back to Venetian times still stands. This most beautiful place in the Ionian sea that is blessed with both mountains and sea, a picturesque combination of green cypresses and blue bays was spared by the devastating earthquake of 1953, which flattened the rest of Kefalonia, and remained intact. For this reason Fiscardo has been declared a traditional and scheduled settlement.

The first thing that impresses visitors, especially if they arrive by boat, is the beautiful architecture of the houses with their tiled roofs and frenzy of colors. Ochre, blue and pink coloured walls mix with the green, blue and red of the shutters. Only under the Junta was this frenzy of colours curtailed, when the inhabitants were forced to paint all the houses, and even the pier, white.

This did not manage to affect however, the joy and love of life. It is not by chance that the first hippies who came to the island in the 60's chose to stay in Fiscardo. They used the lighthouse keeper's house as their home and base. They organized parties playing their guitars and singing in which many foreigners and local people took part. When they decided to "go out" they transferred this festive atmosphere to "Kira Irini's" place.

"Kira Irini's" is a legend for Fiscardo as it was the first place to open and function as a café, a place to drink ouzo and as a restaurant. It was the meeting place of the locals and of the few visitors and was basically the first of many that followed.

During the late sixties and early seventies, the first yachts that were hired in Piraeus, mainly by American tourists, started arriving in Fiscardo. It is during this decade that Fiscardo seriously starts to prepare

itself for the tourist industry by way of fine-looking and fully equipped accommodation, very good restaurants and special coffee bars. It is the young people of the island who are responsible for this transformation and who manage to change the mind of the inhospitable people of Kefalonia and transform Fiscardo into a "doll's house" which does itself up during winter so that for the rest of the year it can welcome those who have loved it and come back every year and those who are coming for the first time, enticed maybe by its fame.

So from May to October many English, Dutch and fewer Germans arrive and, mainly in August, many Italians, either by charter flights or their own yachts or yachts hired from foreign and Greek companies.

When strolling along the harbour the sight of the multi-coloured sails of the anchored boats is beautiful as is that of the sailboats slowly entering the harbour with Ithaca as a background, while you are sipping your coffee as the sun sets. Fiscardo attracts a large number of Greek tourists, who come here to spend all their holidays or for a visit while staying in another part of the island or on a nearby island and who will not leave until they have visited Fiscardo at least once. After swimming, enjoying their lunch and sipping a relaxing drink by the sea and listening to music, some decide that one day is not enough and search for accomodation, which is very difficult, if not impossible to find at that time, especially in August.

Since the early 90's, many famous people, Greeks and foreigners, have adopted Fiscardo as it is a quiet, idyllic place to spend a few days of peace and relaxation away from the maddening crowd and the scores of backpackers who invade most islands.

It is not only natural beauty that keeps visitors in Fiscardo, but also its accommodation, shops and places of entertainment which can cater for most of their needs. They can visit the house where our poet, Nikos Kavadias lived for part of his life and also the Museum of Fiscardo which

was created exclusively by voluntary work and is housed in the old junior school which was renovated and repaired by the Research Center of the Ionian Sea and whose findings are exhibited in the museum.

The RCIS is involved in the protection of the environment and especially in the research of the protected sea turtle Caretta-Caretta, the Pina Nobilis, a very important shellfish and another, equally important, shellfish, the Posidonia Oceanica.

How to get there

Fiscardo can be reached by air with daily flights from Athens to Argostoli or from abroad by direct charter flights. By sea daily from Patras to Sami and from Killini to Poros or Argostoli. Fiscardo is 50km from Argostoli and 40km from Sami. Along the way you can admire the picturesque harbour of St. Efthimia, Mirtos bay with the wonderful colours of its waters and then Asos with its impressive fortress standing on Asos peninsula. There are daily connections from Fiscardo to Vasiliki, Nidri on the island of Lefkada and neighbouring Ithaca. Every day, during summer, there are day trips to and from these islands. Finally, the harbour of Fiscardo has adequate space for the anchoring of a large number of yachts.

Panagis Dendrinos
and Katerina Vasalaki

Local products of Kefalonia

I hope that this introduction of mine will help you to sample and enjoy our local products.

Many companies produce a wide variety of local bottled wines. A lot of these have become well liked and some have distinguished themselves in competitions. Look out for them in factory outlets and supermarkets. Ask for them at restaurants, at off-licences and mainly in shops selling traditional products.

In the villages of Kefalonia, in many houses, you will find exquisite home-made wines and especially in the area of Omalon where you will find the famous Robola which has a yellowy-green colour. In other villages try to find the equally famous Mavrodafni, Vostilidi and Muscat.

The olive oil of Kefalonia is one of the best in Greece. Look out for it at oil-mills and supermarkets and mainly in the villages.

Traditional music

For those who love the local traditional music, look out for tapes in record shops and shops selling souvenirs. Local traditional music clubs can inform you as to where traditional dancing shows are held.

Red mandoles

The most traditional sweet of Kefalonia is the red mandola, which is always served at engagement parties. At weddings there is always a red mandola among the sugared almonds in the boboniera (net pouches) offered to guests.

Caramel mandoles

Another kind of mandola which is less well-known.

Kidonopasto or Komfeto

One of the trees that thrive in Kefalonia is the quince. There are many sweets made from quinces and one of these which can be found in local pastry shops, is Kidonopasto, otherwise known as Komfeto.

Barboule

A local sweet made from honey, sugar, almonds and lemon juice.

Honey

A very special gift for relatives and close friends, the best thyme honey with a unique aroma and special taste.

Soumada

Look out for soumada if you would like a special refreshing drink.

Garlic

Something you should know if you manage to find the real Kefalonian garlic, especially that from the area of Erisos, is that if a recipe for Skordalia calls for three heads of normal garlic, then just one Kefalonian garlic will suffice. The local garlic is relatively small and reddish in colour.

Wild herbs

Some rare fragrant herbs are native to Kefalonia. For the climbing clubs, which come from all over Europe, the sight of these herbs is becoming

rare. Lavender is one of the herbs that you can buy in material pouches or loose and use in your cupboards.

Oregano

If you are lucky enough to find local oregano, your cupboard will acquire a wonderful aroma for a long time. Boiled it makes a tasty beverage.

Savoury or thyme

Readily found in the mountains and often also in low-lying areas very close to the road. If you add a few pieces to some Feta cheese and milk in a container it will give the cheese a wonderful flavour.

Sage

Frequently used in soups; it also makes an exceptionally aromatic hot beverage.

Mint

It used in many foods and it imparts an amazing flavour, especially to pies and meatballs. It also makes a wonderfull hot beverage when boiled.

Cheeses

Cheese-making began in Kefalonia and spread all over Greece and even abroad, especially the making of Feta cheese. The cheese-makers of Kefalonia, and particularly those of the Pylarou area, have worked in the largest cheese dairies of Greece, Italy, Albania and many other countries. Even today they are highly sought-after and well-paid.

Clockwise from left to right: red mandoles,
caramel mandoles, barboule, kidonopasto, a tape
with music from Kefalonia.

ΛΥΚΟΥΡΓΟΣ ΤΖΑΚΗΣ

Feta cheese

The Feta cheese of Kefalonia might be the best in the world although this may sound exaggerated. You can find soft, medium and hard or peppery varieties.

Ladotiri or Graviera

In Kefalonia you will find fantastic ladotiri and graviera whose origins are not totally local.

Saltless mizithra

You will find it in the cheese dairies of Kefalonia of which there are a fair number because they provide a large part of the domestic market as well as the overseas market. For instance, 10 years ago, in Astoria N.Y., I found wonderful cheeses from Kefalonia. Enjoy mizithra on its own, with sugar and cinnamon, with salt or honey, or use it to make pastries. It does not last long because it contains no salt.

Dry mizithra

You can find it in the local markets all year round. Remove the rind and enjoy it as an appetizer or grated over pasta dishes.

Kefalotiri

A local cheese of Kefalonia, hard and peppery, made from full fat milk. Kefalotiri is a hard and peppery white cheese. It can be substituted with Irish Regato.

Clockwise from left to right: honey, soumada, garlic, wild herbs.

Yogurt

You can find the fresh local yogurt in many dairies; it has a slightly sour flavour.

Meat

You can find meat from free-grazing animals on Kefalonia and especially lamb, kid and goat meat. During Easter, Kefalonia provides a large part of the Greek markets with meat. Do not miss trying pork on the spit if you find it in some grill houses of Kefalonia and especially in the mountain villages. If you happen to be in the area of Erisos in search of the best pork on the spit look out for Maki Skiadaresi in Enossi.

Clockwise from left to right: Graviera, kefalotiri, dry mizithra (top centre), Feta cheese (in the mould), saltless mizithra (below centre), ladotiri.

General notes

– The quantity of ingredients is specified when required.

– Cooking times are approximate, as they depend on the quality of the ingredients. A regular saucepan was used.

– When a recipe contains a lot of vegetables, use water sparingly as the vegetables themselves release water.

– Oil the baking dish well for all pie recipes.

–Add the salt to the pulses 10 minutes before the end of cooking time.

–Pulses and water:
   a. Soak pulses overnight in plenty of water – it should more than half fill the container.
   b. In the morning, boil the pulses in double their quantity of water for 5-8 minutes and discard this water.
   c. Boil the pulses a second time in double their quantity of water and if the water evaporates, add 1-2 more glasses depending on how thick you would like the soup to be.

– In the fish salad, potato salad, potato salad with mayonnaise, skordalia, boiled goat, stuffed cabbage leaves, boiled lobster, lamb or young goat fricassee, the water should cover the ingredients. Add an extra 1-2 glasses if required.

– For the fruit in heavy syrup and the jam keep the following in mind:
   a. Add the lemon juice 5 minutes before turning off the heat.

b. To test if the syrup is ready, first pour some syrup onto a saucer and check to see if it thickens and, secondly, allow the syrup to cool for 4-5 hours then test to see whether it has thickened enough. If not, boil it a little longer.

– The recipes for Mayonnaise, Mustard sauce and Pastry for pies are given before the rest of the recipes and are not repeated in any recipe in which they are mentioned. Refer to the relevant pages (42, 44, 46) as necessary.

Mayonnaise

3 egg yolks
1 tsp mustard
salt
white pepper
juice of 1/2 lemon
1 tbsp vinegar
2-2 1/2 cups seed-oil
1/2 coffee cup water

Using a mixer on a low setting or with a wire whisk but always mixing in the same direction, beat the yolks with the mustard, vinegar, salt, pepper and add the seed-oil a little at a time until the sauce starts to thicken.

Towards the end add the water and the lemon juice.

Mustard sauce

800 g olive oil
450 g vinegar
1 tsp salt
1/2 tsp pepper
5 tbsp mustard

Place the olive oil, vinegar, salt, pepper and mustard in a 1 1/2 lt. jar.
   Screw on the lid and shake very well until all ingredients are combined.
   Keep the sauce in the fridge for a long time.
   Shake well before each use.
   It can be used on all green salads, on boiled dried beans, boiled potatoes and anything you think it tastes good with.

Pastry for pies

To fit a 40×35 cm [16×14 in] dish

1 kg plain flour
1 glass olive oil
1/3 glass white wine
1/3 glass vinegar
2 eggs
salt
pepper
lukewarm water
extra flour/cornflour for rolling

Mix all the ingredients together with half the oil to form a dough that does not stick to the fingers.

Roll out three sheets of pastry.

The sheet used to cover the base will be the largest so that it can extend beyond the edges. The middle sheet will be the smallest, so that the overlap can cover it. The top sheet will be the same size as the baking dish.

Brush the ovenproof dish and the sheets of pastry with the remaining oil.

To prevent the pastry from sticking while rolling it out, dredge the work surface with cornflour and flour.

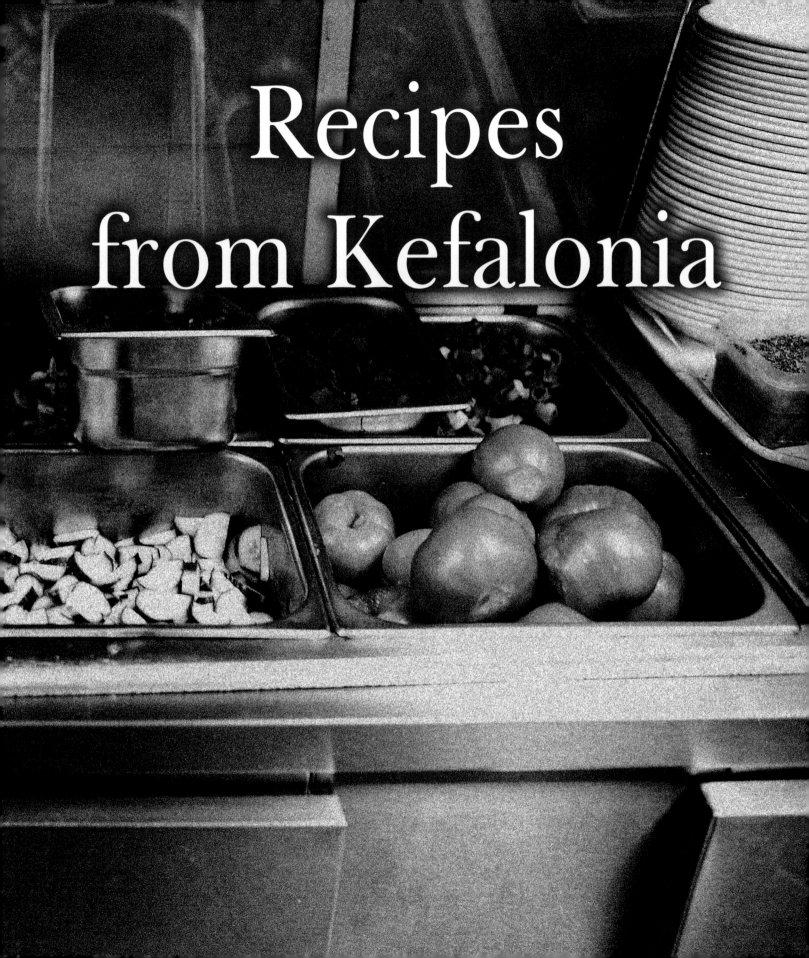

Recipes
from Kefalonia

Cockrel in tomato sauce
with potatoes

1 cockrel (1 1/2-2 kg, cut into portions)
1 glass olive oil
salt
pepper
1/2 glass red wine
1/2 glass tinned tomatoes, finely chopped
1/2 tbsp tomato paste
5-6 cloves garlic, finely chopped
2 medium onions, finely chopped
10-12 pearl onions
1 kg potatoes, peeled
2-3 cloves
1 bay leaf
1 small cinnamon stick
8-10 glasses water

Sauté the cockrel portions in the olive oil in a frying pan, remove them and place in a saucepan.

In the same oil sauté the pearl onions then transfer them to a plate. Add to the frying pan the chopped onion and garlic followed, shortly afterwards, by the tomatoes and the tomato paste that you have dissolved in the red wine. Simmer for 5-7 minutes.

Pour the sauce over the cockrel. Add the salt, pepper, bay leaf, cloves and cinnamon.

Add the water a little at a time and allow to boil for 30 minutes before adding the pearl onions. The cockrel needs to boil for 1 1/2 hours.

Thirty minutes before turning off the heat add the potatoes cut into pieces.

Meat pie

**2.8 kg cubed meat (The meat can be either
beef or lamb. The traditional pie is made
with goat meat. It is a matter of taste.)
2/3 glass olive oil
1/2 glass red wine
salt
pepper
1 tbsp tomato paste
1 glass yellow rice, suitable for pilaf
2 medium onions
5-6 cloves garlic
a little fresh mint
a little fresh oregano
a little fresh dill
a little fresh parsley
pastry for pies
water**

The fresh herbs give the pie a delicious flavour. If you cannot find fresh herbs, use dried herbs but instead of dried oregano use dried basil.

The ingredients are enough for a 40×35 cm [16×14 in] baking dish.

Sauté the finely chopped onion and garlic with the meat. Add the wine, in which you have dissolved the tomato paste.

Add the salt, pepper, water and herbs.

Boil the meat for 1 1/2-2 hours. It depends on the meat. There must be a little liquid left. Add the rice and turn off the heat.

Oil the baking dish and line it with one of the three pastry sheets.

Add the filling. Top with the other two sheets of pastry, and oil them.

Bake in a preheated oven at 170° C [350° F / Gas 3 1/2] for 1 hour.

When the pastry has begun to shrink from the sides, the pie is cooked. Remove the pie from the oven, cover immediately with a clean cloth and leave for 1 hour.

This is a delicious dish, which everyone likes.

"Lagoto" with lamb
or baby goat

2 kg meat, cut into portions
a little flour, for coating
1 glass white wine
1 glass olive oil
1/2 glass vinegar
1 bay leaf
1 tbsp mustard
1 tbsp oregano
salt
pepper
8-10 glasses water
20 cloves garlic, cut into strips

Rinse the meat and coat it in flour. Heat the oil in a frying pan, shake off the excess flour from the meat, and sauté it.

Transfer the sautéed meat to a saucepan. In the same oil, fry the garlic until brown then add the mustard and a little water.

Add this sauce to the meat. Pour in the vinegar and wine and allow the meat to soak them up.

Add the salt, pepper, oregano, bay leaf and water (not too much, 2 glasses to start with then add more).

The meat needs to be boiled for 1 hour 10 minutes-1 hour 30 minutes depending on how young the animal was.

This delicious dish can be served with rice or chips.

Salt cod pie

2 kg thick pieces of salt cod
1 glass olive oil
3-4 white beet
10 spring onions
10 cloves fresh garlic, peeled
parsley
dill
fresh oregano
fresh marjoram
1 tbsp tomato paste
2 fresh poppies
salt
pepper
1/2 glass white wine
1 glass yellow rice, suitable for pilaf
pastry for pies

Soak the cod in water for 28-30 hours changing the water frequently.

Remove the skin and bones. Cut into small pieces.

Sauté the garlic, onion and cod in the olive oil. Add the white wine in which you have dissolved the tomato paste.

Add the herbs and pepper. You may not need salt, so taste the mixture first.

You will need to add very little water to boil, perhaps only 2 glasses since the herbs release their own juices.

Boil everything together for 35-40 minutes.

When there is little liquid left, add the rice. Turn off the heat at once. Oil a 40×35 cm [16×14 in] ovenproof dish, line with a pastry sheet, add the filling and cover with another two oiled pastry sheets. Bake in a preheated oven at 170º C [350º F / Gas 3 1/2] for 50-60 minutes.

Cream cheese pie

900 g unsalted cream cheese
225 g margarine
ground cinnamon for sprinkling
450 g sugar
a little icing sugar for sprinkling
150 g sultanas
1 tbsp cognac
6 tbsp cornflour
pinch of salt
1 tsp vanilla essence
6 eggs
juice and rind of 1 lemon
150 g ground almonds

Beat the margarine, sugar and egg yolks together then add the cream cheese, almonds, cornflour, salt, vanilla, lemon juice and rind and the sultanas previously soaked in the cognac. Finally, add the beaten egg whites.

Bake in a pre-heated oven at 180º C [350º F / Gas 3 1/2] for 50 minutes.

The pie is ready when a knife inserted into it comes out clean. Sprinkle with a little icing sugar and cinnamon.

Potato casserole

1-1.3 kg potatoes
2 medium onions, finely chopped
2/3 glass olive oil
1 glass tinned tomatoes, finely chopped
1 bay leaf
salt
pepper
6-8 glasses water
3-4 cloves garlic, finely chopped
1/2 tbsp tomato paste

Heat the olive oil in a saucepan and add the onion and garlic.

Add the potatoes cut into pieces, the tomatoes, tomato paste and stir them into the oil. Add the bay leaf, salt, pepper and water, a little at a time.

Simmer for 50 minutes.

This is one of the oldest traditional dishes of Kefalonia. It used to be prepared when a family ate meat only once a week and it was a tasty and filling dish.

Tripe soup with tomato

2 kg beef tripe
5 onions (700 g), coarsely chopped
1 glass olive oil
1 kg ripe tomatoes or 700 g chopped tinned tomatoes
1 tbsp tomato paste
2 bay leaves
a few cinnamon sticks
4-5 cloves
5 cloves garlic
juice of 2-3 lemons
salt
pepper
1/2 glass red wine
water

Wash the tripe very well and rub salt and lemon all over it. Let it stand in the lemon juice for quite a while. Blanch it in plenty of hot water then remove and cut into pieces of the desired size.

Pour the olive oil into a saucepan and sauté the onions, garlic and tripe.

Dissolve the tomato paste in the red wine. Add the tomatoes, the tomato paste and wine and enough water to cover the tripe.

Leave to simmer, remembering to replenish the water, and add the bay leaf, cinnamon sticks, cloves and pepper.

It needs to be boiled for a long time, maybe even for 3 to 3 1/2 hours.

10 minutes before turning off the heat, add the salt.

Riganada

1 round loaf of bread
4-5 tomatoes
olive oil
oregano
salt
400-500 g Feta cheese (optional)

In the past, riganada was made with very stale bread which was moistened with water, allowed to drain and drizzled with olive oil, salt and oregano.

We sometimes added sliced tomato so that the bread absorbed its juices and crumbled feta cheese.

Today, as we rarely have stale bread in our homes, when we want to serve riganada, which has now become very fashionable, we can cut thick slices of bread, toast them and prepare them in the same way.

Skordalia – Mashed potatoes with garlic

1 kg potatoes
1/2 glass lemon juice
1 glass fish stock or octopus stock
salt
1 glass olive oil
1 large head garlic (80 g)

Boil the potatoes in their skins in salted water for 45-50 minutes. They need to be very soft.

Beat, in a mortar if you are up to it, or, in a mixer, the potatoes, olive oil, lemon juice and fish stock.

Peel the garlic and chop with a little oil in the blender and add this last, after the potatoes have cooled down a little, otherwise the garlic flavour will become too strong. Add salt to taste.

Do not make the skordalia too dense as it will thicken later.

The recipe from Kefalonia requires that the potatoes be beaten with fish or octopus stock. When octopus stock is used the mixture becomes pink.

Serve skordalia alone or with octopus, salt cod (fried or boiled), or boiled, baked or fried fish, or with any kind of boiled or fried vegetables.

Scrambled eggs

1 small onion
1/3 glass olive oil
100 g Feta cheese
3 ripe tomatoes (450 g)
5 eggs
salt
pepper

Sauté the chopped onion well. Add the finely chopped tomatoes and fry for 5 minutes.

Beat the eggs with the salt and pepper.

Cut the Feta cheese into small pieces.

Add the eggs and cheese to the frying pan. Stir with a wooden spoon until the mixture is cooked through.

Lamb or baby goat offal with eggs

600-700 g offal
2/3 glass olive oil
salt
pepper
3 eggs
100 g kefalotiri

Heat the oil and add the cut up offal. Season with salt and pepper. The offal needs to be fried for 10 minutes.

When it is nearly ready pour off half the oil. Beat the eggs with the kefalotiri and add to the offal. Stir, turning constantly until the eggs are cooked through and serve.

A very quick and especially tasty appetizer.

Boiled goat meat

2 kg goat meat (suitable for boiling)
2 medium onions
3-4 ripe tomatoes
300-400 g celery
1/2 tbsp tomato paste
1 tbsp salt
1/2 tsp pepper
3-4 medium carrots
2-3 courgettes
3-4 medium potatoes

If the meat has come from a recently slaughtered animal leave it in the fridge for 3-4 days before cooking.

Rinse the goat meat well and place in a saucepan with enough salted water to cover it. As soon as the water starts to heat, a froth will form on the surface which should be removed with a slotted spoon.

When the water starts to boil, add the celery, onions, pepper, tomatoes and tomato paste. 1 hour later add the carrots and, after another 30 minutes, the potatoes and courgettes.

The meat can be served with just the vegetables or with small pasta shapes cooked in the broth.

It needs to be boiled for 2 1/4-2 1/2 hours.

Tsigaridi with squid

Skatzili

Kafkalithres

Sorrel

Pourangino

3/4 glass olive oil
1 kg white beet
300 g squid
500 g leeks (small ones if you can find them – preferably wild)
salt
pepper
fresh mint
fresh oregano
fresh parsley
fresh celery
300 g fresh ripe tomatoes
250 g spring onions
dill
2-3 poppies
100 g long grain rice
sorrel (a wild herb which looks like white beet)
2-3 skatzikia (a wild herb)
3-4 kafkalithres
·fresh marjoram
2-3 pourangina (the pourangino is a wild herb,
also named borage and used medicinally)
2 glasses water

The success of this depends on the flavour of the above herbs. If you cannot find some of these, it does not matter. If you do not like squid you can omit it.

Sauté the leeks, spring onions, sliced squid and tomatoes in the oil. Add the herbs and a little water. Boil for 1 hour.

10 minutes before turning off the stove add the rice.

The same ingredients can be used to make a pie.

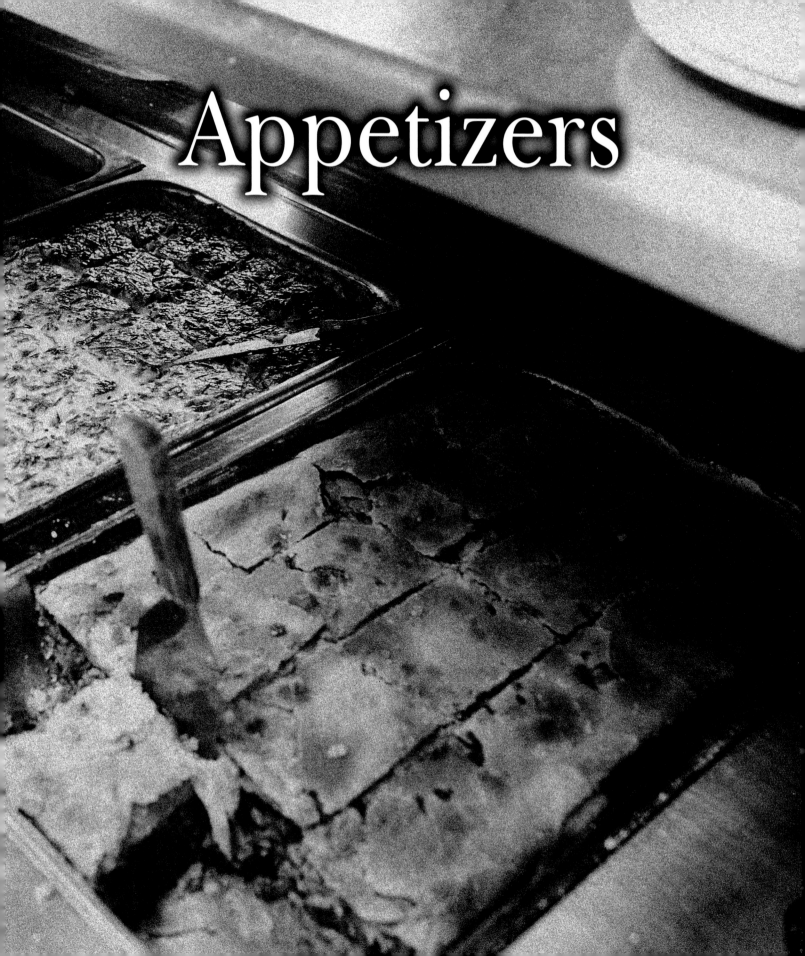

Appetizers

Cheese and ham croquettes

10 egg whites
1/2 kg fillo pastry
1/2 glass water
26-27 slices ham
oil for frying
900 g soft yellow cheese
1 kg grated kefalotiri

Cut the fillo sheets into three after they have thawed.

Cut each slice of ham in two.

Cut the yellow cheese into fingers, (approximately 20 g each).

On each strip of fillo pastry place a slice of ham and piece of cheese then roll into an oblong shape.

Beat the egg whites well with the water.

Dip each croquette into the egg white mixture and roll in the grated kefalotiri.

Deep fry in plenty of very hot oil.

The croquettes are ready when they become golden. They must be served and eaten hot.

Makes 50-54 pieces.

Secret

1. If you do not like ham, use only cheese.
2. If you are planning a special dinner, you can prepare the croquettes a few days in advance and keep them refrigerated until the last minute then just dip them in the egg white mixture and roll in the grated kefalotiri.

Kolokithokeftedes – Baby marrow croquettes

1 1/2 kg baby marrows
1 carrot (100 g)
1 large onion (100 g)
5 cloves garlic
parsley
basil
mint
dill
salt
pepper
4 eggs
300 g of grated rusks
200 g flour
1 tsp ground nutmeg
500 g grated kefalotiri
oil for frying

Grate the carrot and baby marrows and squeeze out as much liquid as possible – this is essential.

Chop the garlic and onion in the blender. Chop the herbs.

Place all the ingredients in a bowl and combine well.

Shape into round croquettes and fry in a shallow frying pan in very hot oil.

Serve hot.

Baked eggplants

2 1/2 kg round eggplants
oil for frying
2/3 glass olive oil
3-4 cloves garlic
350 g Feta cheese
1 1/2 glasses water
salt
pepper
parsley
dill
5-6 onions (600-700 g)
600 g chopped tinned tomatoes or 1 kg fresh ripe tomatoes
1/2 tbsp tomato paste

Slice the eggplants and soak in salted water for approximately 1 hour. Drain and fry them the evening before; leave to drain overnight in a colander.

Heat the olive oil in a deep frying pan or saucepan. Sauté the onion and garlic. Add the tomatoes, tomato paste, salt, pepper, parsley, dill and water. Allow the sauce to thicken.

Lay the eggplants in an ovenproof dish. Pour the sauce over them and top with the Feta cheese cut into pieces.

Bake in a preheated oven, at 180º C [350º F / Gas 4], for 1 hour.

Eggplant patties

1 kg large, long eggplants
oil for frying

For the coating

3 eggs
200 g grated rusks
200 g flour

For the filling

1 egg
200 g grated Feta cheese
100 g kefalotiri
50 g Edam
150 g dill
1/2 glass olive oil
250 g flour
1 tin evaporated milk
1 glass water
salt
white pepper

Beat the egg in the cold water. Heat the oil, add the flour and let it cook. Add the milk and previously beaten egg. The mixture should be golden brown.

Allow to cool then add the rest of the filling ingredients.

Cut the eggplants into long, thin slices and lightly fry.

Roll the filling into oval shapes placing one oval on each slice of eggplant. Wrap up and roll each piece in flour. Dip into the beaten eggs then roll in the grated rusks. Dip once more into the beaten eggs and fry in plenty of oil.

Makes 50 pieces.

Serve hot.

Tzatziki – Yogurt dip

**1 kg Greek-style yogurt
1 cucumber (300 g)
1 small carrot
10 cloves garlic, minced
1/2 tbsp salt
pepper
dill (optional)
3 tbsp olive oil
2 tbsp vinegar**

Grate the washed cucumber with its skin and the carrot.

Squeeze out as much liquid as possible from the cucumber and carrot.

Mix them into the yogurt then add the vinegar, oil, garlic, salt, pepper and dill (if used).

Cheese pies

1 kg fillo pastry, thawed
oil for frying

For the béchamel sauce

3 tbsp vegetable fat
1/2 glass seed-oil for the sauce
salt
pepper
1/2 tsp nutmeg
2 glasses plain flour
500 g Feta cheese
4 eggs
250 g yellow cheese
250 g kefalotiri
3 glasses evaporated milk
2 glasses water

To prepare the béchamel sauce heat the vegetable fat and seed-oil and add the flour stirring well so that it cooks and does not form lumps.

In a separate saucepan, heat the milk with the water, salt, pepper and nutmeg. Add this to the flour mixture a little at a time stirring continuously removing the pan from the heat.

When the sauce thickens, add the eggs, beaten, and the cheeses.

Cut the fillo pastry into 3 strips. Place 1 teaspoon of filling on the lower part of each strip and fold into triangles.

Fry the cheese pies in hot seed-oil. Allow to drain in a colander before serving.

Note

If you do not wish to fry the cheese pies the same day, keep them in the freezer, in layers separated by cotton cloths. An all-time favorite. One of the tastiest appetizers for Greeks and foreigners.

Htipiti or tirokafteri – Cheese dip

500 g Feta cheese
2 tbsp water
1/2 glass olive oil
4 tbsp vinegar
1 hot red pepper

Beat everything together in a blender.
A very tasty appetizer, especially if served with toast.

Salads

Tassia's salad

1/2 iceberg lettuce
1 bundle rocket (or 1/3 finocchio)
1 carrot, cut into matchsticks
1 small cucumber, cut into matchsticks
1 medium tomato
1/2 red bell pepper, sliced
15-20 mini (cherry) tomatoes
1 tbsp capers
5-6 large olives
tender leaves of 1-2 lettuces
1/2 glass mustard sauce

Place the washed and drained greens in a deep glass bowl. Add the capers, the tomato cut into quarters, the mini tomatoes, olives and red pepper.

Arrange the carrot and cucumber matchsticks around the sides.

Pour the mustard sauce over the salad.

Eggplant salad

2 kg large dark-coloured eggplants
2-3 cloves garlic, minced
1/3 glass olive oil
2-3 tbsp vinegar
salt
pepper
parsley, finely chopped
50 g walnuts, coarsely chopped (optional)

Bake the eggplants at 200º C [400º F / Gas 6] for 1 hour and 10 minutes.

Peel and place in a colander and leave to drain.

Place in the mixer with the rest of the ingredients and blend.

Potato salad

1 kg potatoes
salt
2/3 glass mustard sauce
1 medium onion or 3-4 spring onions
3 gherkins
15 pieces of capers
parsley
3-4 boiled eggs

Boil the potatoes in their skins in salted water for 35-40 minutes.

Peel the potatoes and while they are still hot, put them into the sauce to soak it up.

Add the chopped onion, gherkins, capers and last of all the parsley so that the potatoes will have cooled and the parsley does not soften.

Cut the eggs in half and place next to the potatoes or on top of them and serve.

Potato salad with mayonnaise

1 kg potatoes
salt
pepper
1-2 onions (300 g)
400 g mayonnaise
1 tbsp mustard
parsley

Boil the potatoes in their skins in salted water for 35-40 minutes, peel and dice.

Chop the onion and parsley and add the salt, pepper, mayonnaise and mustard.

Mix into the potatoes.

The potato salad can be kept in the fridge for 6-7 days.

Horiatiki – Greek salad

1-2 medium tomatoes (300 g)
1 small onion
1/2 green pepper
6-8 olives
1/2 cucumber
100 g Feta cheese
oregano
2 tbsp olive oil
1 tbsp vinegar (optional)

Cut all the ingredients (except the olives) into pieces and arrange in a dish with the tomatoes first, then the onion, pepper, cucumber and finally the Feta cheese. Add the olives. Before serving, sprinkle with oregano, salt, olive oil and vinegar.

Fish salad

900 g fish suitable for boiling
(Cod is very good or Monkfish)
1-2 onions (200 g)
500 g mayonnaise
2 carrots (200 g)
salt
pepper
2 potatoes (250 g)
100 g gherkins
150 g celeriac
150 g peas
25-30 pieces of capers
350 g tuna in oil

Blanch the peas for 10 minutes. Drain the tuna. Chop the gherkins and capers. Boil the fish with the vegetables, salt and pepper for 40 minutes

Bone the fish and chop the boiled vegetables. Mix together with the rest of the ingredients.

This very tasty dish can be served either as an appetizer or as a main course accompanied with a green salad.

Pulses
Rice

Gigantes – Broad beans in tomato sauce

1/2 kg broad beans
1 glass olive oil
water
2 carrots (200 g)
celery
a little dill
3-4 onions (400 g)
1 tbsp salt
1/2 tsp pepper
1 tbsp tomato paste

Soak the beans in lukewarm water overnight. The next morning, boil them in the same water for a while, remove, then place in a saucepan with fresh water and add the rest of the ingredients except for the salt, which should be added only at the end.

Boil the beans for 40 minutes then transfer to an ovenproof dish and bake for a further 40 minutes.

Chickpea soup

1/2 kg chickpeas
salt
pepper
1 glass olive oil
1 medium carrot
1 medium onion
celery
water

Soak the chickpeas overnight in lukewarm water.

　Boil them in the same water and discard it. Pour in enough fresh water to cover the chickpeas and add the oil, celery, onion, pepper and carrot.

　Boil for 3 hours. 10 minutes before turning off the heat, add the salt.

Note

To reduce boiling time, 1 tsp. bicarbonate of soda can be added to the water for soaking, in which case the chickpeas should be rinsed very well afterwards.

Rice and vermicelli

1/2 kg yellow rice, suitable for pilaf
1 lt water or chicken or beef stock
1 tsp salt
1/2 tsp pepper
50 g butter
1/3 glass olive oil
100 g vermicelli

Heat the vermicelli with the oil and butter. The vermicelli must turn golden. Add the water or stock.

When the water boils, add the rice, reduce the heat and leave to boil for 20 minutes until all the water has been absorbed.

Fakes – Lentil soup

1/2 kg lentils
1 glass olive oil
1 bay leaf
4-5 cloves garlic
1/2 tsp oregano
water
salt
pepper
1-2 fresh tomatoes (300 g) or
1/2 glass tinned tomatoes, chopped (optional)

Boil the lentils and discard the water. Place them in the saucepan with fresh water, add the rest of the ingredients and boil for about 1 hour. A little vinegar may be added when serving, if liked.

Fasolada – Dried bean soup

1/2 dried beans
1 glass olive oil
1/2 tbsp salt
pepper
1 potato (200 g)
2 carrots (250 g)
1-2 onions (200 g)
celery
water
2/3 tbsp tomato paste
1/2 green pepper (optional)
2-3 hot chili peppers (optional)

Soak the beans in plenty of lukewarm water, overnight.

The next morning, drain them and boil in fresh water for 5 minutes, drain once more and discard the water.

Place the beans in a saucepan with more water. Add the oil, pepper, tomato paste, sliced carrots, chopped potato, celery, onion and peppers if used.

Finally, 10 minutes before the soup is ready, add the salt.

Boil for 1 hour 40 minutes to 2 hours.

Fish
Seafood

Pasta with lobster

1 lobster (1-1.3 kg)
2/3 glass olive oil
salt
pepper
3 bay leaves
water
2 glasses tinned tomatoes or 800 g ripe fresh tomatoes, finely chopped
1/2 glass cognac
basil (fresh if available, otherwise dried)
fresh parsley to garnish
800 g pasta (any shape you like, however, it is worth finding the homemade
pasta called "milelia" which is delicious)
2 medium onions, finely chopped
2-3 cloves garlic, finely chopped
1 coffee cup vinegar

Fill a saucepan with plenty of water and add the salt, vinegar and 2
bay leaves. When the water comes to the boil add the lobster and cook
for 10 minutes. Remove the lobster and reserve the cooking water.

Heat the oil and sauté the onion and garlic. Add the cognac then
the tomatoes, salt and pepper and 1 bay leaf.

Allow the sauce to thicken slightly and pour in the water (3-4 glasses) a little at a time as required during boiling (40 minutes). Ten
minutes before turning off the heat, add the lobster cut into portions of the desired size without discarding anything.

Stir the lobster into the sauce and finally add the basil.

Boil the pasta in the water having strained it first through a cloth
as the lobster sometimes releases sand when boiled.

The pasta should be al dente. Drain then mix with the
sauce. Sprinkle with chopped parsley and serve.

This dish has recently become very fashionable and you
are sure to find it prepared in many different ways.

Boiled lobster

1 lobster (approximately 1 kg)
water
salt
1 bay leaf
1/2 glass vinegar

Place the water, salt, vinegar and bay leaf in a saucepan.

When the water starts to boil, add the lobster and cook for 20-25 minutes.

Cut in half with a strong knife.

Serve hot or cold with oil and lemon or mayonnaise.

Note

Boil for 10-12 minutes for every 1/2 kg of lobster.

Kakavia – Fish soup

1 small lobster
1 rock perch
1 dragonet
1 cod
1 grouper
(approximately 1/2 kg each)
1 bay leaf
a medium sized cuttlefish
8 glasses water
juice of 3-4 lemons
1 small ripe tomato
1 medium onion
2-3 cloves garlic, unpeeled
2 medium carrots
celery
5-6 medium potatoes
1 glass olive oil

Boil the water, olive oil and all the remaining ingredients except for the fish and lemon juice.

After the vegetables have been boiling for 15 minutes add the fish allowing 5-6 minutes between each kind; the tougher ones first then the softer ones such as the cod. Do this so that all the fish are evenly cooked.

The fish needs to be boiled for 20-25 minutes.

Five minutes before turning off the heat, add the lemon juice.

Note

Kakavia is a dish made from various fish suitable for boiling. It is the most traditional dish for fishermen.

I tried to give an indication of the kinds of fish that may be used.

Fried squid

1 kg squid
salt
oil for frying
flour for coating

If the squid is fresh, it is advisable to keep it in the deep freeze for 5-6 days before frying, so it softens, especially the eyes, and does not splatter during frying.

Heat plenty of oil in a deep frying pan.

Salt then flour the squid, and place in the hot oil. Do not put too many in at once and do not fry for very long so that it does not dry out.

Serve hot.

This is one of the few dishes that are prepared better in restaurants than at home and it delights both children and grown-ups, Greeks and foreigners.

Stuffed squid

4 squid approximately 400-500 g each (preferably fresh)
1/2 glass olive oil
1/2 glass wine
1 glass yellow rice, suitable for pilaf
1/2 tbsp tomato paste
parsley
salt
pepper
3 glasses water
2-3 cloves garlic
1 medium onion

Prepare the squid by pulling the head upwards so that you do not damage the body. Rinse it well.

Finely chop the garlic, onion and a few squid tentacles. Sauté in oil. Add the wine in which you have dissolved the tomato paste.

Rinse the parsley.

When the sauce has reduced, add 1 1/2 glasses water.

As soon as it boils, add the rice and turn off the heat.

Leave the rice to swell a little. Fill the squid using a teaspoon and sew up the opening with a thick needle and thread so that the stuffing does not come out.

There will be some rice and tentacles left over.

Place the stuffed squid in a baking dish together with the left-over rice and tentacles and add approximately 1 1/2 glasses water.

Bake in a pre-heated over at 170º C [350º F / Gas 3 1/2] for 1 hour 10 minutes.

Fisherman's pasta

200 g finely chopped squid
200 g finely chopped cuttlefish or octopus
200 g mussels, shelled
10-12 whole mussels
2 hot chili peppers
1 bay leaf
salt
red pepper
15 medium prawns, shelled
10-12 cockles (if available)
3-4 cloves garlic
1 large onion
2/3 glass olive oil
1/3 glass cognac
2 glasses finely chopped tinned tomatoes or 800 g fresh tomatoes
parsley
700 g pasta (any kind)*
3-4 glasses water

Sauté the garlic and onion in the oil.

Add the squid, cuttlefish or octopus and the chili pepper and continue to sauté. Pour in the cognac.

Add the tomatoes and allow the juices to evaporate.

Add the bay leaf, salt, pepper and, little by little, the water and leave to simmer for 40-50 minutes.

10-12 minutes before turning off the heat add all the mussels and, five to six minutes later, the prawns and cockles (if available). Do not reduce the sauce too much because the pasta will be added to it.

Undercook the pasta slightly because after draining it will be added to the sauce and soften as it absorbs some of the liquid. Serve hot in a large platter and garnish with a few whole mussels and cockles from the sauce.

Sprinkle with finely chopped parsley.

A delicious dish. Very summery. Almost everyone will be sure to like it.

---

*The best pasta for this dish is penne (quill shape pasta).

Fried salt cod

1 piece salt cod
oil for frying
flour for coating

Soak the cod for 30 hours changing the water frequently.
Cut it into portions and remove the scales.
Roll in the flour and fry in hot oil.
Served, if liked, with skordalia.

Boiled octopus

1 octopus (1-1 1/2 kg)

1 glass white wine
olive oil
2 bay leaves
oregano
very little water (if required)
vinegar

Taste the octopus before adding salt as it has a lot of salt of its own. It also contains a lot of water, so very little additional water or even none at all will be required during boiling.

Place the octopus in a saucepan with the wine and bay leaf. The saucepan must be covered well. Simmer over low heat for 1-1 1/4 hours.

Prick the octopus to see if it is ready.

When cooked, add a little oregano, vinegar and oil.

Serve with skordalia or on its own as an appetizer.

Keeps for several days in its own juices with oil and vinegar.

Note

If fresh octopus is used it is essential that it be well beaten and kept in the deep freeze for a couple of days before cooking.

Octopus casserole

1 1/2-2 kg octopus, cut into portions
1 medium onion, finely chopped
2 bay leaves
2-3 cloves garlic, finely chopped
very little salt
pepper
1/2 glass wine
1 glass tinned tomatoes, finely chopped
1/2 tbsp tomato paste
1 kg pearl onions, peeled
1 glass olive oil
4 glasses water

Scald the octopus in boiling water then cut into pieces. It is much easier to cut when blanched.

Heat the oil and sauté the pearl onions then place in a bowl.

In the same oil sauté the finely chopped onion and garlic.

After a while add the octopus and leave to sauté before adding the wine in which you have dissolved the tomato paste and, a little later, the salt, pepper, bay leaf and finely chopped tinned tomatoes.

Pour in the water a little at a time and leave to simmer for 1 1/4- 1 1/2 hours.

Thirty minutes after it has started bubbling add the pearl onions.

A very tasty and impressive Greek dish.

Boiled fish

1 1/2-2 kg fish, suitable for boiling
2 large carrots
2 medium onions
4-5 medium potatoes
2-3 courgettes (if available)
1 glass olive oil
the juice of 3 lemons
salt
pepper
celery
8 glasses water

Place the olive oil, water, salt, pepper and vegetables in a saucepan to boil.

If using a whole fish, or a large piece of fish, add this too to the saucepan.

If using several small fish, boil the vegetables for 15 minutes before adding the fish.

The vegetables and fish should be boiled for 40 minutes.

Five minutes before turning off the heat add the lemon juice.

Serve the fish and vegetables with the broth in a separate bowl.

This is a very easy dish, which many of your friends will like, whether they are Greeks or foreigners.

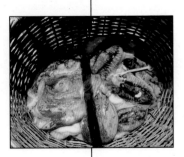

Meat
Poultry

Meatballs

1 1/2 kg minced beef
3 eggs
200 g ground rusks
1/2 tsp pepper
1/2 tsp oregano
1 tbsp salt
parsley, finely chopped
fresh or dried mint
1/2 glass milk
1/2 glass water
flour for coating
2 tbsp vinegar
2/3 glass olive oil
2-3 onions (300 g), finely chopped
7-8 cloves garlic, minced or finely chopped
oil for frying

Mix all ingredients together. Put a little oil in a saucer to oil the palms of your hands while you roll the meatballs.

Heat some oil in a frying pan.

Roll the meat balls in the flour and fry for 5-7 minutes.

It is advisable to change the oil half way through.

Makes approximately 60 medium meatballs.

Kleftiko

1 leg of meat (lamb or kid), approximately 1 1/2 kg
10-12 cloves garlic
2 medium carrots
1.3-1.5 kg potatoes
150 g kefalotiri, cut into strips
salt
pepper
suet (from 1 lamb or kid), if available
4-5 sheets greaseproof paper
water

Salt and pepper the meat, prick the leg with a knife and insert the garlic and kefalotiri in the holes.

Cut the potatoes and carrots into pieces, salt and pepper them, add a few garlic cloves and pieces of kefalotiri, and wrap in the suet, if using. Lay out the greaseproof paper, place the meat on it next to the potatoes and carrots (wrapped in suet or not) and fold into tight parcels.

Preheat the oven to 250º C [475º F / Gas 9].

Fill a baking tin 2/3 full with water and add the parcels. Bake for 2 1/2 hours, replenishing the water continuously.

When cooked, serve on platters, in the greaseproof paper which should be slit open.

Individual portions can be prepared in the same way.

This is a delicious dish, which gets its flavour from the garlic. So if you do not like garlic do not attempt it.

Chicken in the oven

1 chicken, 1.5-1.7 kg
1 1/2 kg potatoes
2-3 medium lemons
salt
pepper
oregano
8 cloves garlic
2/3 glass olive oil
1-2 glasses water

1st variation

Cut the chicken in half. Peel and cut the potatoes into long pieces. Salt and pepper them both. Add the oregano, oil, lemon and garlic.

Place in an ovenproof dish with a little water and bake in the oven at 180° C [350° F / Gas 4] for 1 hour 40 minutes, or until cooked, turning over after 50 minutes.

2nd variation

The chicken can be baked whole, stuffed with salt, pepper, oregano, garlic, kefalotiri and pepper. Pour the lemon juice over it.

The baking time is about the same.

Additional ingredients: **1/2 green pepper**
100 g kefalotiri

Stuffed cabbage leaves

1 kg minced beef
7 eggs
4 lemons (to make 1 glass lemon juice)
salt
pepper
1 tbsp cornflour
dill
150 g long grain rice
2 medium onions, finely chopped
1 glass olive oil
2 medium carrots
celery
water
2 cabbages (4 1/2 kg)

Mix the minced beef with 2 whole eggs, rice, a little olive oil, a little dill, one onion and a little water and roll into 34-35 rounds.

Bring a large, deep saucepan of salted water to the boil. Cut off the stem of the cabbages, so that the leaves come away easily.

Place the cabbages in the boiling water. The leaves will soon start to separate. Take each leaf and roll around a meatball.

Layer the bottom of a saucepan with the carrots, sliced onions, celery and the medium-sized cabbage leaves, which are too small to stuff.

Lay the stuffed cabbage leaves on top of these and add water. Boil for 1 hour.

A short while before turning off the stove, beat 5 egg yolks with a little water. Add some of the juice from the saucepan, the lemon juice and cornflour. Turn off the heat and pour in the egg and lemon sauce.

Egg yolks alone are used to prevent the sauce from curdling.

Boiled beef with egg and lemon sauce

2 kg beef, suitable for boiling
celery
3 eggs
3-4 medium carrots
3-4 medium lemons
1 medium onion
salt
pepper
1 glass long grain rice
water

Boil the meat in salted water and skim off the froth.

Continue boiling and add the pepper and onion then the celery and, 1 hour later, the carrots. Do not add them from the beginning as they will become too soft and dissolve.

The meat needs to be boiled for 2-3 hours.

Strain the broth and allow 1 glass of rice per 6 glasses of broth. If you do not have enough broth, top up with water.

Allow the broth to boil and add the rice. Do not boil for more than 10 minutes.

For the egg and lemon sauce

Separate the egg yolks from the whites.

Beat the whites, add the yolks, a little water, the lemon juice and the broth a little at a time.

Turn off the heat and add the egg and lemon mixture to the rice while stirring the rice in the same direction.

Makes about 4-5 bowls of soup.

Beef in tomato sauce

1 kg beef, suitable for stew
1 kg beef bones
1 1/3 glasses olive oil
salt
pepper
6 cloves garlic, finely chopped
3-4 cloves
500 g onions, finely chopped
1 bay leaf
1 tbsp tomato paste
500-600 g tinned tomatoes or fresh ripe tomatoes, finely chopped
1/2 glass red wine
8-10 glasses water

Beef bones are needed to enhance the flavour during boiling.

Pour the oil into a frying pan, cut the beef into 5-6 pieces and sauté. Transfer to a saucepan together with the bones.

Place the onion and garlic in the frying pan to sauté.

Add the tomatoes and the tomato paste dissolved in the red wine.

Empty all into the saucepan with the meat and season with the salt, pepper, bay leaf and cloves.

Add the water a little at a time and boil for 1 hour 30 minutes-2 hours.

Whole leg of pork in the oven

1 leg of pork, boned, approx. 4 1/2 kg
6-8 cloves garlic
salt
pepper
oregano
150-200 g kefalotiri
1 tbsp mustard
4 glasses water

Ask your butcher to bone a whole leg for you. Use a sharp knife to slice down the middle without reaching the edges.

Cut the garlic into strips and mix with the salt, pepper, oregano and mustard. Spread this mixture on the inside and outside of the pork.

Cut the kefalotiri into long strips and stuff the meat with it. Place in an ovenproof dish with water that should be replenished during cooking and bake at 200° C [400° F / Gas 6]. As the meat takes a long time to cook (3 hours) cover it with tin foil. If liked, potatoes may be added 1 hour before the end of the cooking time. They become very tasty.

Allow the meat to cool before cutting. Serve as a main course or cold platter. It provides many servings when sliced.

Lamb or young goat fricassee

1 1/2 kg meat
2 large lettuces
juice of 3 lemons
3 eggs
dill
2-3 sticks celery
10 spring onions
1 glass olive oil
water
salt
pepper

Rinse the lettuces, cut them into thick strips and blanch in boiling water. Place in a colander.

Chop the spring onions, celery and dill.

Heat the oil, rinse the meat, cut it into portions and sauté. Add the onions and fry lightly until softened. Place everything in a saucepan with a little water, the celery, salt and pepper.

Thirty minutes later add the dill and lettuces.

The meat does not need to be boiled for longer than 1 hour 30 minutes.

When the food is cooked and very little liquid is left, turn off the heat, add the egg and lemon sauce and stir.

For the egg and lemon sauce

Beat the egg whites with a little cold water. Add the yolks, lemon juice and a little hot liquid from the food.

Desserts

Tassia's dessert

750 g Greek-style yogurt
250 g fresh cream
1 tbsp icing sugar
1 tbsp cognac
200 g jelly (the same flavour as the tinned fruit used)
1 can tinned fruit, mixed or pineapple or any other kind (800 g)
2 glasses water

1st variation

Beat the fresh cream with the icing sugar and cognac.
Drain the fruit reserving the syrup. Cut the fruit into small pieces.
Dissolve the jelly in boiling water and remove from the heat.
Mix the yogurt, jelly, cream, fruit pieces and syrup together. Pour this mixture, which will be runny in the beginning, into any kind of dish you like: baking tin, bowls or glasses. Refrigerate for 2 hours.

2nd variation

This dessert is delicious with strawberries during the strawberry season. Instead of tinned fruit use 1/2 kg strawberries and 200 g strawberry jelly.
The amount of water should be 4 glasses since there is no syrup.

Note

When using tinned fruit, add as much water as required to the juice from the tinned fruit to make it up to 4 glasses.
If fresh strawberries are used, 2 tablespoons of icing sugar should be added to the fresh cream prior to beating.

Yogurt with toasted almonds
and fruit in heavy syrup

1 kg Greek-style yogurt
1 cup coarsely chopped almonds, toasted
1 cup fruit in heavy syrup

In a deep glass bowl place the yogurt, then the fruit and finally the almonds.

A delicious dessert, good for the digestion and a quick solution for an impromptu dinner. Sometimes the simplest dishes are also the most tasty.

Orange biscuits

1 glass olive oil
1/2 glass seed-oil
2/3 glass fresh orange juice
1/3 glass fresh lemon juice
1 coffee cup cognac
1 glass sugar
1 tsp bicarbonate of soda
1/2 tsp ground cinnamon
1 tsp baking powder
1/2 tsp ground cloves
1 pinch salt
1 kg plain flour
1 tsp sesame seeds (optional)
grated rind of 1 tangerine

Beat the olive oil, seed-oil, sugar and tangerine rind in the blender. Combine the bicarbonate of soda and baking powder with the flour.

After the oil has been well beaten, empty the mixture into the mixer bowl with all the remaining ingredients adding the flour last.

The dough should not stick to the fingers. Form into various shapes.

Bake in a preheated oven at 170º C [350º F / Gas 3 1/2] for 35-45 minutes. The biscuits are ready when they turn golden brown. To make sure, taste one. Allow to cool. Store in an airtight tin or glass container.

This is an easy recipe. It always turns out well and is much liked.

Kourambiedes
– Almond shortbread crescents

600 g fresh butter, at room temperature
400 g vegetable butter, at room temperature
1 1/2-2 kg plain flour
1 1/2-2 kg icing sugar
2 egg yolks
1 glass coarsely chopped almonds
1 coffee cup ouzo*
1 tsp bicarbonate of soda
2 tsp baking powder
salt

Beat the butters well with 4 tbsp of the icing sugar and the egg yolks. Add the ouzo and the almonds.

Weigh out 1 kg flour and add the baking powder, bicarbonate of soda and salt to it. Add the flour mixture to the butter mixture then as much of the remaining flour as required to make a dough that does not stick to the hands. Shape into crescents and bake in a pre-heated oven at 170º C [350º F / Gas 3 1/2] for 40 minutes. As soon as you take the kourambiedes out of the oven, and while they are still piping hot, sift the icing sugar over them. Do not remove them from the baking sheet until they have cooled completely because they will break.

Taste one to make sure they are cooked. Makes approximately 60 medium size crescents.

Note

These are traditional Greek Christmas biscuits and in some areas such as Lefkada they are made for all happy and festive occasions throughout the year.

---

*Ouzo is a Greek aperitif with a strong aniseed flavor.

Caramel cream

For the cream
4 tins evaporated milk
4 tins water
juice and peel of 1 orange
1 tsp vanilla essence
1/2 kg sugar
20 eggs

For the caramel

1/2 kg sugar
1/2 coffee cup water
juice of 1/2 lemon

To prepare the caramel

Place all the ingredients in a frying pan or saucepan and brown to taste. To see the colour, place a little of the caramel on a saucer.

To prepare the cream

Beat the eggs in a mixer at a very low speed and for a very short while.

Heat the milk, sugar and vanilla essence together with the orange peel which should later be discarded. Do not let the mixture boil.

Remove the milk from the heat and pour the eggs into it through a fine sieve stirring continuously.

While the caramel is still hot use it to coat several individual moulds or one large one. After it has cooled down slightly, add the cream.

Place the moulds or mould on a baking dish contains approximately 2 1/2 cm (1 inch) water.

Preheat the oven to 250° C [475° F / Gas 9], put in the moulds then reduce the heat to 180° C [350° F / Gas 4] and bake for 1 hour. The cream is ready when a knife inserted into it comes out clean.

This recipe makes about 30 individual moulds.

Quinces in heavy syrup

5 kg quinces
sugar
juice of 2 lemons
2 lemons
water
cloves
blanched and toasted almonds

Peel the quinces and remove the pips. Boil the quince peel and pips with a little water. Cut the quinces into the desired shape and size and place in cold water with lemon juice so that they do not brown.

They should now weigh approximately 3 1/2 kg.

Boil the peel and pips for 15-20 minutes.

Weigh the quince pieces and place them in a saucepan with an e-qual weight of sugar.

From the juice produced by boiling the peels and pips measure 2/3 of a glass for every 2/3 kg of prepared quince and strain.

Pour it into the saucepan with the quince pieces, add a few cloves and boil for 40-50 minutes. Five minutes before turning off the heat pour in the juice of the 2 lemons.

To test if the syrup is ready, pour a little onto a saucer. When the quinces are cool, add the almonds.

Baked quinces

1 1/2 kg quinces
2 glasses sugar
1 cinnamon stick
cloves
3 glasses water

Wash the quinces well and cut in half. Remove the pips and the hard core, place these in a saucepan with the sugar and water and boil for 8-10 minutes.

Stick 2 cloves into each quince half and place in an ovenproof dish.

Strain the juice that the pips and core boiled in and pour it into the ovenproof dish with the cinnamon.

Bake in a pre-heated oven at 180º C [350º F / Gas 4]-200º C [400º F / Gas 6] for 1 1/2-2 hours.

A little juice should be allowed to remain as it turns into a very tasty quince jelly when cold which can be served with the quinces. Accompany with whipped cream, if liked.

Loukoumades

1 kg plain flour
enough dry yeast for 1 kg flour
juice of 1 lemon
juice of 1 orange
1/2 tsp salt
3 tbsp sugar
lukewarm water
oil for frying
toasted sesame seeds for sprinkling
ground cinnamon for sprinkling
1/2 kg honey

Make the dough one hour before you plan to fry the loukoumades. Dissolve the yeast in a little lukewarm water. Add the lemon juice, orange juice, salt, sugar, flour and enough water to obtain a runny dough.

Keep the dough in a warm place covered with a blanket.

The dough will double in size. When you are ready to fry the loukoumades heat the oil in a saucepan, take a handful of dough and with a wet teaspoon cut off small pieces and drop them into the oil.

The dough must turn golden brown. Serve sprinkied with honey, cinnamon and toasted sesame seeds.

Note

If you want to get people to come to your place there is no phrase more magical than "Come over, I'm making loukoumades". If you invite 10 people you will get 15 at least.

Nectarine jam

1 kg large nectarines
1 kg sugar
1/2 glass water
1 tsp vanilla essence
1 coffee cup cognac
juice of 1 lemon

Wash the nectarines and cut into large pieces. Boil them with the sugar for 30-40 minutes.

Five minutes before turning off the heat, add the vanilla essence, lemon juice and cognac and mix well.

Melomakarona

1 glass olive oil
1 glass seed-oil
1/2 glass sugar
1/2 glass beer, at room temperature
1/3 glass cognac
pinch of salt
ground cinnamon
ground cloves
ground nutmeg
1 tsp bicarbonate of soda
2 tsp baking powder
1 glass ground almonds
1 1/2 kg plain flour, approximately
juice and zest of 1 orange

For the syrup

1 1/2 glasses honey
3 glasses sugar
1 cinnamon stick
2 glasses water
10 cloves
juice of 1/2 lemon

For sprinkling

Finely chopped almonds mixed
with cinnamon and a little sugar

Beat the olive oil, seed-oil and sugar together well.

Add the salt, beer, cognac, a little cinnamon, cloves and nutmeg and the orange rind and juice.

Mix the bicarbonate of soda and baking powder with the flour and add to the oil mixture. Finally, add the almonds.

The dough is ready when it does not stick to the fingers.

Shape into ovals and bake in a pre-heated oven at 180º C [350º F / Gas 4] for 40-45 minutes. Remove and set aside. When the biscuites have cooled, boil all the syrup ingredients together for 10 minutes and, keeping the syrup boiling, dip each melo-macarono in it for 1-2 minutes. Remove and sprinkle with the almond mixture.

Taste one to make sure they are cooked. Makes 60-65 pieces.

Rice pudding

1 glass pudding rice
1 glass sugar
6 glasses water
6 glasses milk
1 pinch salt
3 tbsp cornflour
1 piece lemon peel
ground cinnamon
3 eggs

Boil the water and rice with a pinch of salt for approximately 12 minutes. Beat the eggs, sugar, lemon peel, cornflour and 1/2 glass milk with a mixer.

Add the rest of the milk to the boiling rice when the water has reduced. Boil for 5-7 minutes. Lastly add the egg mixture.

Stir for 2 minutes then turn off the heat.

Pour into individual bowls. Makes approximately 10 bowls. Sprinkle with cinnamon, if liked.

Grapes in heavy syrup

1 kg seedless grapes
750 g sugar
juice of 1 lemon
4-5 cloves

Clean and rinse the grapes. Place in a saucepan with the sugar and cloves.

Boil for 30-40 minutes.

5 minutes before turning off the heat, pour in the lemon juice.

Firikia* compote

2 1/2 kg firikia, peeled
2.2 kg sugar
2 1/2 lt water
1 cinnamon stick
cloves
1/2 glass cognac
juice of 1 large lemon

Stick 2 cloves into each firiki.

Boil all the ingredients together for approximately 1 1/4 hours. 5 minutes before turning off the heat, pour in the cognac and lemon juice.

---

*A firiki is a small apple, the size of a medium egg, with a strong aroma and flavour.

Halvah

2/3 glass seed-oil
1/3 glass olive oil
2 glasses semolina (1 1/2 glasses coarse grained and 1/2 glass fine grained)
almonds
seedless raisins
ground cinnamon for dusting

For the syrup

5 glasses water
3 glasses sugar
juice and zest of 1 orange
1 cinnamon stick
5-6 cloves

To make the syrup, place the water, sugar, cinnamon stick, cloves, orange juice and orange zest in a saucepan.

Boil the syrup for 5-8 minutes.

In another saucepan heat the oil well and add the semolina.

The more you sauté the semolina the darker it will become.

Add the almonds and, when they have coloured, add the raisins.

Pour some of the syrup into the semolina a little at a time.

It is advisable to protect one's hands with an oven glove at this stage, as the mixture will splash upwards.

Pour in the rest of the syrup.

Remove the saucepan from the heat while the mixture is still slightly runny, as it will thicken later.

Cover the saucepan with a clean cloth and leave for a while.

Transfer the halvah to several individual moulds or one large one.

Sprinkle with ground cinnamon.

"Thank-yous"

I honestly thank God, because he may have given me more than I deserve or, in other words, because maybe other people who had the same abilities as myself, perhaps even more, have not managed to achieve as much as I have.

They may not have had a father and mother like mine who, despite our daily confrontations, will always be beside me and support me whenever I need it.

I thank my brothers, who step aside to let me take centre stage and who may have given me more credit than I'm worth; my husband, who is willing to humour me day and night; my daughter, a divine creature, who adores and admires her mother.

In addition, I thank my few but select friends who are always there for me; my few, but loyal colleagues and more than anyone, my customers who have supported us all these years, who have loved us and trusted in us completely; not to mention those people who have used their influence in the media to promote us and make us known extensively, both in Greece and abroad.

And, although it may sound strange or exaggerated, I also thank my few enemies because the confrontations we had awoke my obstinacy and pride which made me stronger and determined to achieve the best. I honestly believe that we owe part of our success to our greater or lesser enemies.

We would like to thank the following companies for their kindness in providing materials and equipment used in the photographs:

Habitat
Leoforos Kifisias 250, Halandri. Tel.: 6778880
Leoforos Poseidonos 67 and Alimou, Alimos. Tel.: 9889000

www.home.com
Spefsippou 7, Kolonaki. Tel.: 7238442, 7258036. Fax: 7258037
Levidou 16 & Argyropoulou 1-3, Kifisia. Tel.: 6233520, 6234046. Fax: 6233521
Omirou 10 & Stratigi 7, Psychico. Tel.-Fax: 6721710
Pentelis 10, Halandri. Tel.: 6831820
Karolou Dil 20, Thessalonica. Tel.: 031-284157. Fax: 031-284135

Studio Kosta Boda Illum
Stadiou 19, Athens. Tel.: 3252814. Fax: 3226217
Leoforos Thiseos 106, Kallithea. Tel.: 9536572-3. Fax: 9520022
Agias Paraskevis 8, Halandri. Tel.: 6838191-2. Fax: 6843864
Levidou & Argyropoulou, Kifisia. Tel.: 8010068. Fax: 8017428
Tsimiski 95, Thessalonica. Tel.: 031-241927. Fax: 031-241591

OUZO 12. Ouzo with history. Ouzo with Greek soul.

Constantinople 1880

As far back as 1880, the customers of Kaloyiannis Distillery, who appreciated a fine ouzo always insisted on being served from "Barrel No 12". This ouzo was the result of selected seeds and herbs which were blended harmoniously and which underwent a double distillation process resulting in an exceptional ouzo with a rich flavour and fine aroma.

Thessaloniki 1925

Some years later, the Kaloyiannis family moved to Thessaloniki. Naturally it didn't take long for the ouzo from "Barrel No 12" to become famous here as well...

Piraeus 1950

This exceptional ouzo and its fine reputation were destined to travel once more, this time to Piraeus. It was at that time that Kaloyiannis first bottled his ouzo, giving it the name "OUZO 12" in honour of the famous Barrel. It was in fact the first ouzo ever to be bottled in the customary "karafaki" (small carafe), a move that was destined to establish the way in which ouzo is consumed in Greece today.

English translation by: PANAYOTA VLAHOPOULOU – DANIELLE BOWLER
Editors: TONIA CHOURCHOULI,
MARIA GOURNIEZAKI, VASSIA ANTONOPOULOU
Copy editor: DANIELLE BOWLER
Typesetting, design and layout, cover, printing:
LIVANI PUBLISHING ORGANIZATION S.A.
Cover plastification: I. CHARAMARAS
Bound by: VASSILIS KYPRAIOS – IOANNA TSIAKA
Head of production: KONSTANTINOS ZACHARAKIS
Head of distribution: KOSTAS MARKOPOULOS